MADRIGALI

MADRIGALI

BY
T. A. DALY

AUTHOR OF
"CANZONI," "McARONI BALLADS,"
" CARMINA"

**PICTURES BY
JOHN SLOAN**

WILDSIDE PRESS

To
BRENDA

PROEM

TO A CORRESPONDENT

MY favorite poet? I'm afraid
    You'll sneer at my selection;
And if "a poet's born, not made,"
    It may deserve rejection.
'Tis true his puny stature shows
    The lines that he is built on
Much less heroic are than those
    That moulded
                      Milton.

I grant you may with Byron's fame
    Crush my poor bard's to jelly,
Or dim his rush-light in the flame
    That wreathes the name of
                      Shelley.

Behold him, too, in thought or style
    Not even Burns' or Blake's peer—
Poor pigmy piping many a mile
    In rear of
                      Shakespeare.

Yet not for any one of these
   Great names that loom above him
W ould I exchange those qualities
   That make me fondly love him.
I love his living heart that sings
   And makes my blood flow faster;
I love so many little things
   Of which he is the master.
I love his ardent joy of life,
   And, faith—as I'm a sinner—
I love his bairns, his home, his wife,
   His appetite for dinner.
My favorite poet? I'll rejoice
   And tread this old earth gaily
As long as I can hear the voice
   Of
                      T. A. Daly.

CONTENTS

	PAGE
PASQUALE PASSES	3
SPRING IN THE BLOOD	6
NARCISSUS	8
THE BLOSSOMY BARROW	10
THE WISE MAN O' BEAUFORT	12
THE WEDDING ANNIVERSARY	15
W'EN KITTY KANE OBLIGES	17
THE LAGGARD IN LOVE	20
THE WHISPERERS	22
THE TWO BLIND MEN	25
DREAMING	27
THE STUDENT	29
THE CROWS	31
THE GIFT O' THE GAB	32
TONY MARATT'	34
THE OULD LAD O' THE BELLS	36
THE KNOWIN' NICODEMUS	39
THE YOUNG WIDOWER	41
THE END O' THE DAY	43
SAN PATRICE	45
AN INTERPAROCHIAL AFFAIR	47
THE ITALIAN WIND	49
L'UNIVERSALE NOTA	51

	PAGE
The Vestibule	52
Rosa's Parrakeets	54
Da Spreeng-Charmer	56
Girls Will Change	60
W'en Spreeng Ees Com'	62
April's Wizardy	64
The Fallen Tree	66
Da Faith of Aunta Rosa	68
Waiting for the Train	70
Padre's Peencha Snuff	72
The Scouts of Spring	74
A Song of Tonio	77
The Wandering Minstrel	78
Paradise Regained	80
April	82
Easter Eve	84
The Temperamental Tommasso	85
The Butt o' the Loafers	87
A Ballade of Brides	89
Da Greata Basaball	91
The Man's the Man	94
Da Summer's Com'	96
Da Thief	98
What the Flag Sings	101
Ballade of Summer's Passing	103
Sanctuary	105
Shawn Bhui O'Connor	107
Italian Lesson	109
Artful Young Barney Kehoe	111
Leigh Woods Near Bristol Town	113

	PAGE
CHATTERTON	116
KERRY UNVISITED	117
MR. HAIL COLOMB'	120
OCTOBER SONG IN ROMANY	121
THE MAGIC APPLE	123
A SONG TO GIULIA	125
THE TIDES OF LOVE	126
WHEN DORANDO BEAT HAYES	127
THE ABSENT-MINDED SHE	128
W'AT'SA "NORAYSUICIDE?"	129
DA NO-GOOD WORKAMAN	131
OCH!	134
THE GOLDEN GIRL	135
LABOR'S SABBATH	137
A CHILD'S CHRISTMAS SONG	139
UNDER THE HOLLY	141
A CHRISTMAS CAROL	142
DA COLDA FEET	144
SONG OF THE CHRISTMAS TREE	146
DA POLEETICA BOSS	148
THOUGHTS OF ROSA	150
OULD MATT'EW MORAN	152
IL GRILLO	156
THE ONE THING LACKING	158
BUSINESS DIPLOMACY	160
AN IDYLL OF OLD JOYS	162
FINER CLAY	166
THE CHRISTMAS READING	168

ILLUSTRATIONS

"Giuseppe da barber ees crazy weeth Spreeng"		Frontispiece
"I no can bust up soocha beautiful theeng"		facing page 10
"Sittin' in the corner wid their elbows on their knees"	"	" 22
"Now I mus' leeve for da Madre"	"	" 34
"Rosa, weeth her parrakeets"	"	" 54
"She justa pray, an' pray, an' pray"	"	" 68
"Yerra! boys will have their play"	"	" 88
"Wan leetla rose stuck een her hair"	"	" 98
"Mother and wife to me, fostering Earth!"	"	" 122
"You theenk for sure dey growin' dere"	"	" 132
"Show how you vote jus' by maka da cross"	"	" 148
"Those pictures old, but ever new"	"	" 168

MADRIGALI

PASQUALE PASSES

ROSA Beppi she'sa got
  Temper dat's so strong an' hot,
Ees no matter w'at you say,
W'en she's start for have her way
She's gon' have eet; you can bat
Evra cent you got on dat!
Theenk she gona mind her Pop?
She ain't even 'fraid of cop!
Even devil no could stop
Rosa Beppi w'en she gat
Foolish theengs eenside her hat.
Dat'sa why her Pop ees scare',
Dat'sa why he growl an' swear
W'en he see her walkin' out
Weeth Pasquale from da Sout'.

Eef, like Beppi, you are com'
From da countra nort' of Rome,
You would know dat man from Sout'
Ain'ta worth for talka 'bout.
Ees no wondra Beppi swear,
Growl an' grumbla lika bear.
W'en da Padre Angelo

Com' an' see heem actin' so,
He's su'prise' an' wanta know.
Beppi tal him. "Ah!" he say,
"I weell talk weeth her to-day,
So she stoppa walkin' out
Weeth Pasquale from da Sout'."

Beppi shak' hees head an' sigh.
He don't theenk eet's use for try,
But da Padre smile an' say:
"I gon' speak weeth her to-day."
Pretta soon, bimeby, he do—
Only say wan word or two—
But so soon as he ees through
You should see da Rosa! My!
Dere's a fire from her eye,
Cutta through you lika knife.
She ees mad, you bat my life!
But no more she's walkin' out
Weeth Pasquale from da Sout'.

Beppi's gladdest man I know
W'en he see how theengsa go.
"My!" he say, "I am su'prise'
Church can be so strong an' wise."

"Yes," say Padre Angelo,
"Church ees always wisa so.
All I say to her ees dees:
'Rosa, I am moocha please'
Dat at las' you gotta beau.
He ain't verra good wan, no;
But you need no minda dat
Seence he's best dat you can gat.
So I'm glad for see you out
Weeth Pasquale from da Sout'.' "

SPRING IN THE BLOOD

IF, when spring is in the blood,
    ('Tis of Irish blood I'm speakin')
All the peace o' bachelorhood
    Glad ye'd be to be forsakin'
        For the hope o' joy that lies
        In a pair o' sparklin' eyes
            Wishful to possess ye,
        Take your chance o' paradise
        An' Heaven bless ye!

If, when spring is in the blood,
    Grosser appetites awaken,
An' ye feel a thirst that could,
    Maybe, bear a little slakin'—
        If to clear your throat o' dust
        Mountain-dew will ease ye, just—
            Sure, I'd never chide ye.
        Take your tipple if ye must,
        An' Wisdom guide ye!

If, when spring is in the blood,
    Weary on your toil, ye're wishin'
You could wander through the wood

Where the other lads are fishin';
If such sport as ye could know
Where the Irish rivers flow
    Waters here can lend ye,
Seize your day of pleasure; go,
    An' Luck attend ye!

If, when spring is in the blood,
    Play-boy pranks nor eyes o' woman
Stir your heart-strings as they should,
    Faith, ye're somethin' less than human!
What ye need's another birth;
Though, indeed, 'twould not be worth
    All the trouble to remake ye.
Fit for neither heaven nor earth,
    The Divvil take ye!

NARCISSUS

ONE night, while yet the wold
    Lay dormant with the cold,
I flung the casement wide
And, pausing ere I drew
The outer shutters to,
    A lovely thing espied—
A thing of precious worth,
A bit of heaven in earth—
        A star in water.
Beneath the rose-bush bare
A rain-pool glassed it. There,
    By its own beauty glamored,
It poised above the brink,
Flashed down and seemed to sink
    To darkness, self-enamored.

That vision of delight
Oft walked my dreams at night.
    Lo! now 'tis fructified!
This morning when I rose
And scanned my garden close,
    What marvel I espied!
A wonder of new birth,

A bit of heaven in earth—
    A star in blossom!
Beneath the rose-bush bare
It braves the chilly air,
  With beauty's self to bless us;
Spring's herald true!   Behold,
With horn of gleaming gold,
    The heaven-born Narcissus!

THE BLOSSOMY BARROW

ANTONIO Sarto ees buildin' a wall,
But maybe he nevva gon' feenish at all.
Eet sure won'ta be
Teell flower an' tree
An' all kinda growin' theengs sleep een da Fall.

You see, deesa 'Tonio always ees want'
To leeve on a farm, so he buy wan las' mont'.
I s'posa som' day eet be verra nice place,
But shape dat he find eet een sure ees "deesgrace;"
Eet's busta so bad he must feexin' eet all,
An' firs' theeng he starta for build ees da wall.
Mysal' I go outa for see heem wan day,
An' dere I am catcha heem sweatin' away;
He's liftin' beeg stones from all parts of hees land
An' takin' dem up to da wall een hees hand!
I say to heem: "Tony, why don'ta you gat
Som' leetla wheel-barrow for halp you weeth dat?"

"O! com' an' I show you w'at's matter," he
   said,
An' so we go look at hees tools een da shed.
Dere's fina beeg wheel-barrow dere on da
   floor,
But w'at do you s'pose? From een under
   da door
Som' mornin'-glor' vines have creep eento
   da shed,
An' beautiful flower, all purpla an' red,
Smile out from da vina so pretty an' green
Dat tweest round da wheel an' da sides da
   machine.
I look at dees Tony an' say to heem: "Wal?"
An' Tony he look back at me an' say: "Ha!
I no can bust up soocha beautiful theeng;
I work weeth my han's eef eet tak' me teell
   spreeng!"

Antonio Sarto ees buildin' a wall,
But maybe he nevva gon' feenish at all.
     Eet sure won'ta be
     Teell flower an' tree
An' all kinda growin' theengs sleep een da
   Fall.

THE WISE MAN O' BEAUFORT

I MIND the day I went away, away from
    Beaufort town,
  With passage money in my purse, but little
    else beside
These two strong hands I meant one day to
    lay on Fortune's frown
  And twist the fickle face of her till it was
    smiling wide.
Not there among the Kerry hills could such
    a task be done,
  Not there where freedom's self had slept
    five hundred years and more,
With each day, from the rising to the setting
    o' the sun,
  As like the one to follow as the one that
    went before;
Where young men trod their fathers' heels
    contentedly and dreamed,
  Nor ever strove for greater wealth or
    knowledge or renown
Than blessed the master o' the school—John
    Kearney—who was deemed

The wisest and the richest man in all o'
    Beaufort town.

With hopes and fears these many years I've
    toiled in foreign lands,
    And cheek by jowl with Poverty trudged
        on behind the plough,
But these two restless hands o' mine, these
    bare, work-hardened hands
    That plucked the frown from Fortune's
        brow are filled with money now.
And knowledge deeper than the kind that
    ever scholar read,
    Or master ever taught from books in quiet
        study hall,
I've gathered through the passing years
    within this grizzled head,
    All ready there for instant use whatever
        need may call.
Small wonder, then, that I, for wealth and
    wisdom widely famed,
    Would smile a pitying smile betimes at
        thought o' the renown
Of Master Kearney there at home, that all
    the neighbors named
    The wisest and the richest man in all o'
        Beaufort town.

To-day I roam where once was home. Back
   here in Beaufort town
  I walk the old, familiar ways, but, O!
   the bitter change;
For out o' tune with everything I wander up
   and down,
  A stranger to the neighbor-folk, whose
   very speech is strange.
The great wide world I fought until it
   yielded me its gold
  Has put its mark upon me, and it will not
   let me rest.
I look with sorrow on the hills that never
   more can hold
  Contentment for the restless heart that
   beats within my breast.
And so for all my wealth and fame, for all
   my presence here,
  John Kearney o' the little school, who
   prates of verb and noun,
And has no care for anything beyond his
   narrow sphere,
  Is still the wisest, richest man in all o'
   Beaufort town.

THE WEDDING ANNIVERSARY

EEF, mebbe so, you gotta wife
   Dat's good as mine to me,
You weell be glad for mak' her life
   So happy as can be.

Las' fall Carlotta tak' my han'
An' maka me so happy man;
Wan year to-day she ees my mate,
An' so to-night we celebrate.
You theenk I would forgat da day
Dat pour sooch sunshine on my way?
Ah! no, I gona lat her see
How kinda husban' I can be;
How glad I am she ees so true,
How proud for all da work she do.
An' so for mak' her work for me
More easy dan eet use' for be,
An' show how mooch my heart ees stir'—
I buy a leetla geeft for her.

Carlotta got so pretta hair,
I buy her som'theeng nice for wear—

Eh? W'at? O! no, ees notta hat;
Ees som'theeng mooch more use dan dat.
Eet's leetla pad, so sof' an' theeck
An' stuff' weeth wool, dat she can steeck
On top da hair upon her head,
So lika leetla feathra bed.
Eet sure weell mak' her feela good
W'en she ees carry loada wood;
An' mebbe so eet halp her, too,
For carry more dan now she do.
So mooch weeth love my heart ees stir'
I buy dees leetla geeft for her.

Eef, mebbe so, you gotta wife
   Dat's good as mine to me,
You, too, would try for mak' her life
   So happy as can be.

W'EN KITTY KANE OBLIGES

OH! youse kin talk erbout de style
   Mis' Patti useter fling,
An' how she'd make youse cry or smile
   To hear de songs she'd sing.
She may be all de highbrows claim,
   She may be great fur fair,
But Music is an open game;
   It ain't no solitaire.
An' dough she played to one night stan's
   W'at panned out t'ousands clear,
She never got no round o' han's
   As honest an' sincere
As shakes our Social's clubroom w'en
   We pass de woid along:
" 'Sh! Mister Mackin's lady frien'
   Is goin' ter sing a song."

My lady frien'! Her steady gent!
   I sit down be her side,
A-playin' her accomp'niment
   An' boinin' up wit' pride.

Me concertina seems ter know
  De woik it's got ter do;
No udder time de notes would flow
  So musical an' true.
An' den she starts ter sing. O, boys!
  I would'n' miss a note
Uv all de melted tears an' joys
  W'at ripples frum 'er t'roat.
An' foist me heart seems choked an' den
  It's jumpin' good an' strong
W'en Kitty Kane, me lady frien',
  Obliges wit' a song.

"De songs My Mammy Sang ter Me,"
  Dat dere's my favoryte;
A pooty song it is, an' she
  Kin sing it outer sight.
Foist off she goes a-warblin' t'rough
  De laughin', jinglin' rhyme,
An' den, no matter w'at youse do,
  Youse can't help pattin' time.
Den suddint comes de solemn part—
  Her sweet voice trimbles so,
It builds an ice house 'roun' yer heart
  An' tear-tanks overflow.

An' den yer back to eart' agen,
  A-cheerin' loud an' long,
W'en Kitty Kane, me lady frien',
  Obliges wit' a song.

O! Kitty Kane, how long! how long!
  I'll on'y be content
W'en youse have sung yer weddin' song
  Ter my accomp'niment.

THE LAGGARD IN LOVE

OH! Giuseppe da barber ees crazy weeth
    spreeng!
He's no good een da daytimes for doin' a
    theeng
But to theenk of da night an da tunes he
    weell seeng.
Alla time w'en som' customer gat een hees
    chair,
He's so slow weeth da shave an' weeth cuttin'
    da hair,
Dat hees boss ain't do notheeng but grumble
    an' swear.
But Giuseppe no care
    For wan blessa blame theeng,
        But to play mandolina
        Where som' signorina
    Weell listen at night to da love-song he
    seeng.

Com' Giuseppe da barber last nighta too late
To da house of da Rosa an' stan' by da gate,
An he seeng like Il Gatto dat cry for hees
    mate.

Soocha playnta love-music, sooch cooin',
    sooch sighs,
Soocha sounds from da heart—an' sooch
    looka su'prise
W'en he leeft hees face up an' stare eento
    my eyes
Lookin' down from da wall!
    Ah! Giuseppe, your call
        Should be starta more earla
        For catcha my girla,
    For w'en da spreeng's here *I* no workin'
        at all!

THE WHISPERERS

Look at ould Mag Carmody an' Anastasia Moore,
  Sittin' in the corner wid their elbows on their knees;
Wid their bony backs bent over an' their worn hands clasped before,
  An' the two white heads together like a pair o' buzzin' bees.
Wasps, more like, you'd call them, for the talk your fancy hears
  Passin' now between them wid a sting in every word,
Talk, ye think, would have the neighbors tinglin' at the ears,
  Wid the heat of anger an' resentment if they heard.
    So, if you'd your way,
    Faith, belike, you'd say:
  "Rise up, whisp'rin gossips, rise!
  L'ave your scandals an' your lies;
Time enough for bitterness when wintry days befall.

But the year is at the spring,
Joy an' kindness are a-wing;
Even wasps are Mayin' now upon the sunny wall."

Look upon the whisperers again—an' hang yer head;
Look upon them kindly, for not long you'll know their likes.
These are of the troublous days whose whisperin' was bred
By the roar o' tyrant guns an" clash o' patriot pikes.
Innocent an' simple is the talk that now they make,
Chat of olden buried things, for thoughts of age are long.
They've no need to whisper, still a habit's hard to break,
An' wid two to nurse the same, sure they keep it strong.
So, if you'd be kind,
Thus you'll speak your mind:
"Rise up, dear ould women, rise!
Here you're under friendly skies;

Come an' take your fill o' talk an' share the
  genial sun.
Here the year is at the spring,
Joy and kindness are a-wing;
Come, forget the bitterness o' days that's
  dead an' done.

THE TWO BLIND MEN

GOOD avenin' to ye, Father; will ye be
    to bide a minyit?
'Tis a week o' weeks since ye was here
    before.
There' manny feet goes up the sthreet, an'
    once yer own was in it—
Last night I heard yer footsteps pass me
    door.
Och! musha, Father, who am I to stop a
    soggarth passin' by
To wan that needs him more?

Aye! "Conor o' the Brooms." I know; he
    bragged of it this mornin',
Wid a dale o' windy wurrds, "sez I,"
    "sez he."
Ye may go bail he'd make the tale, wid
    fanciful adornin',
As wonderful as anny tale could be.
Sure, Father, 'tis mesel' that's glad ye wint
    to cheer yon poor ould lad,
That's blinder far nor me.

O, yes, there *is* a differ, though, I'm free to
    be admittin',
Ways, the two of us is blind as anny stone.
But times, ye see, Con sez to me: "I feel
    so blind jist sittin'
    Wid no wan nigh, jist sittin' by me lone."
They're blind indeed, poor souls, that need
    another's mind to see and read
    What thoughts are in their own.

So ye needn't think I'm jealous of a lad like
    poor ould Conor,
    Fur me own mind's stored wid company
    galore.
An' 'tis little I'll be carin'—though I thank
    ye fur the honor—
    If ye're passin' by or stoppin' at me door.
Sure, ye're welcome, Father Mack, but I'd
    nivver call ye back
    From wan that needs ye more.

DREAMING

I HATE to read of millionaires,
  Because such reading seems
To hypnotize me utterly
  And start me dreaming dreams.
How many times I've figured out
  What I'd be apt to do
If I were in that fellow's place
  And had a million, too.
Of course, I'd use my fortune well;
  More sensibly than he,
For I'd give ten per cent. at least
  To worthy charity.
Another ten per cent. would go
  To help along a few
Of my deserving relatives
  Whose bills are overdue.
And then my duty to the church;
  Of course, a goodly share—
Say, twenty-five per cent. or so—
  Would be devoted there.
I'd give this latter quietly,
  Insisting that my name

Must be withheld, that none might know
    Whence this donation came.
I'd only let the pastor know—
    He'd have to know, you see—
Because my name upon the check
    Would show it was from me.
Another twenty-five per cent.
    Would do myself and wife;
The income we'd derive from that
    Would keep us both for life.
Then, after that—well, after that
    I dream away and plan
To spend still other ten per cents.
    To help my fellow-man.
And finally my dreaming gets
    A bit confused, and then
I take a tumble and my feet
    Touch solid earth again;
And common sense assures me, as
    It stops me with a jerk,
I've wasted time enough to do
    A dollar's worth of work.

THE STUDENT

SPEAK not weeth Dagoman dat sweep da
    street;
  He ees too domb, Signor.
All sense he got ees een hees han's an' feet,
  Jus' dat an' notheeng more.
You laugh for hear heem talk an' mak'
    meestak',
  But, com', eef you would see
How smart som' Dago ees seet down an'
    mak'
  Som' leetla talk weeth me.
Com', let us talk of wiṣa theengs we know.
  So, now I weell baygeen:
Ees eet not strange, my frand, how aard-
    varks grow
  An' keep from gattin' theen?
Eet mus' be tough for eatin' ants an' sooch
  So like dese aard-varks do;
You bat my life, I would no like eet mooch,
  No more, I s'pose, would you—
W'at? "Aard-vark?" Sure! Eh, w'at ees
    dat you say?
  Som'theeng you nevva heard?

O, yes, "a-a-r-d-v-a-r-k;"
   Dat's how ees spal da word.
Eet ees een book, da wisa book I read
   Dat tal all theengs you want.
Ees call' "da 'Mericana Cyclopaed;"
   I buy we wan las' mont'.
An' lasta week I learn da firsta page;
   Nex' week I learna two.
You bat my life, w'en I am good old age
   I gon' know more dan you.
I am su'prise' how mooch you don'ta know;
   You are not smart, Signor.
Ah, wal, good-bye! Com' back een week or so,
   I learn you som'theeng more.

THE CROWS

Caw! caw! caw!
  When last we heard their cry,
  These prophesying crows,
They flecked a leaden sky,
  South-blown before the snows;
And down the whistling wind
Came winter's woes behind
      Their caw! caw! caw!
Ne'er swelled a feathered throat
With half so sad a note.

      Caw! caw! caw!
The South hath blown them back.
  With many a flashing wing
The blue's rain-sweetened track
  Is augural of spring;
Again from out the sky
Floats down the raucous cry
      Of caw! caw! caw!
But where's the feathered throat
That hath a gladder note?

THE GIFT O' THE GAB

OCH! there was ne'er such a quare
    twisted crayture
        As Shaemus McNabb.
Irish in name an' by birth, but by nature
        A surly ould crab.
"Silence is goolden," sez he, "an' 'twill lessen
    the
Most of our throubles here." Och! 'tis
    disthressin', the
Way he's malignin' that chief Irish blessin'—
    the
        Gift o' the gab!

"Silence!" sez he. An' ye ralely can't
    blame us,
        Who're proud o' the gab,
If, now an' then, we go afther this Shaemus
        An' give him a jab.
"What then," sez I, "would we win Irish
    freedom wid?
Chasin' the British out, what would ye
    speed 'em wid?

Dried Irish tongues would ye fatten an' feed
  'em wid,
      Shaemus McNabb?"

"Silence!" he roars; "will ye never be quiet?
    Ye blather an' blab,
Stirrin' the counthry to murther an' riot
    Wid gift o' the gab!"
So will he argue by night an' by day wid you,
Roarin' an' fightin' to have the last say wid
  you.
"Silence!" sez he—Och! the Divvil fly 'way
  wid you,
      Shaemus McNabb!

TONY MARATT'

TONY Maratt' eesa yo'ng 'Merican,
    Born an' raise' up een dees beautiful
       lan'.
Padre from Genoa, madre from Rom',
Long tima seence to dees countra ees com'.
      Nevva mind dat!
Look at heem now! From da sola hees feet
      To da toppa hees hat,
Mos' evrawhere dat you walk een da street
Here ees mos' styleesh yo'ng man you can
    meet—
      Tony Maratt'.

Strong ees dees Tony Maratt', like hees Pa.
Ah! but hees heart eesa sof', like hees Ma.
So seence las' year, w'en hees padre ees die,
Tony Maratt' ain't do notheeng but cry.
      W'at you theenk dat?
"Padre ees worka too hard for hees pay,
      An' jus' see w'at he gat!
My! eet ees sad he should go deesa way;
Now I mus' leeve for da madre," ees say
      Tony Maratt'.

Madre Maratt', now da padre ees dead,
Gotta work harda for maka da bread.
Tony ees sad for da padre, but steell
Jus' for da madre he tryin' to feel
          Happy an' fat.
"Don'ta be scare', leetla madre," say he,
          "I no die lika dat.
I ain't gon' workin' at all, for, you see,
You ain't got nobody lefta but me—
          Tony Maratt'."

THE OULD LAD O' THE BELLS

HARK!
    The bell o' St. Mark,
      How it moithers the air!
    Sure, I can't un'erstand
    All the bells in this land—
      I declare
      But it's quare—
Whin the bells o'er the sea are so joyous an' grand.

    Now, whin I was a boy,
      By the town o' Clonmel,
    I drank nothin' but joy
      From the rim of a bell.
    Was it rung for two wed,
      Was it summons to prayer,
    Was it tolled for wan dead,
      Still the music was there;
    Every hillside an' glen,
      Every hollow an' glade

Rang agen an' agen
  Wid the echoes it made.
An' the good folk that trod
  To the call o' the bell
Gave a "Glory to God!"
  For whatever befell.
Don't I mind—bless me soul!
  Me a wee curly head—
How we heard the bells toll
  Whin O'Connell was dead?
I can mind that same day,
  Aye! I see mesel' well
As I stopped in me play
  At the sound o' the bell;
An' I hold in me ear
  All its music that's past,
Tho' it's sixty-odd year
  Since I heard it the last.
For I can't live it down,
  An' I hear it ring yet
O'er the bells o' this town,
  Wid their tears an' regret—

    Hark!
The bell o' St. Mark,
  How it moithers the air!

Sure, it ought to be gay,
'Tis a weddin', they say—
    I declare
    But it's quare—
An' the bells o'er the sea are so joyous alway.

THE KNOWIN' NICO-
DEMUS

MOST aggervatin' critter wuz old Nico-
demus Brown;
He knowed it all an' bound to have his say.
Thar wuzn't no theayter-play thet ever come
to town
But Brown he'd git to see it night or day.
He'd make a p'int to git his seat 'fore any o'
the rest,
An when the curtain riz upon the show
An' all the actors sot to work, he'd do his
level best
To figger how the plot wuz goin' to go.
An' when the most excitin' part of all wuz
gittin' near,
An' folks wuz settin' narvous an'
perplexed,
Old Brown he'd whisper loud enough fur
every one to hear:
"I'll bet ye I kin tell whut's comin' next."

Thar wuzn't any curin' him. He'd do the
same in church,

Or anywheres he happened fur to be;
Fur, like a dern poll-parrot hoppin' round
    upon its perch,
  He'd squawk to all his critics: "Talk is
    free!"
But when the Typhoi' wuz around last
    August wuz a year,
  It tackled onto Nick an' tuck him down;
An' then he got religion, fur he tho't his end
    wuz near,
  An', sure enough, thet wuz the end o'
    Brown.
His folks wuz gethered by his bed, an' jest
    afore he died,
  While Deacon Jones wuz readin' of a text,
The sick man smiled, an', "Waal, I'm done
    with this here life," he sighed;
  "I'll bet ye I kin tell whut's comin' next."

THE YOUNG WIDOWER

"YOU do not weep," the childless
    woman said.
The babe stirred in his arms; he shook his
    head:
  "I have outworn my grieving.
Better than tears I pledge my sainted dead—
    Devotion to the living."

"A costly life. Your wife you would
    prefer——"
"Have done! I would prefer," he said,
    "for her
  A truer sympathizer
Than you, who often boasted that you were
    Unnaturally wiser."

"I came to sympathize, and yet it's true—"
"Ah! yes," he said, "and when my grief was
    new
  Your words *did* come to taunt me.
But I have need of nothing now from you—
    You cannot cheer or daunt me."

"Yet I may mourn for Womanhood——"
   He said:
"Aye! mourn for that—to-night, beside your
    bed,
   For Womanhood be grieving—
Not Womanhood triumphant in the dead,
   But throttled in the living."

THE END O' THE DAY

Here's the end o' the day,
   An' this weary ould planet
Turns again to the gray,
   Dewy dusk that began it.
An' meself that's no more
   Nor a midge or a flea
Or a sand o' the shore,
   Who'd be thinkin' o' me
     At the end o' the day?

Here's the end o' the day,
   An' it's little I'm winnin'
Wid my toilin' away
   Since the same was beginnin';
But for all I'm so small,
   Trudgin' on by my lone,
If no evil befall
   I've a world o' my own
     At the end o' the day.

Here's the end o' the day,
   An' the stars, growin' bolder,
Now the sun is away,
   Peep above the hill's shoulder;

An' 'tis they that can see
That the dusty boreen
Is a king's road for me
To my castle an' queen,
At the end o' the day.

SAN PATRICE

NOW w'en spreengtime ees baygeen
    Geeve da grass eets tendra green,
An' da sweetness to da air,
Lees'en to my leetla prayer,
    San Patrice!

Een da lan' from w'at I came
Ees not manny speak your name;
Ees not manny call you great,
Like een dees Unita State',
Where all know w'at eet ees mean
W'en dey wear da beet of green
    Lika dees.
See da reebbon on my breast,
Jus' da sama like da rest?
    San Patrice!

Pleass, I ask you, San Patrice,
Mak' da green be flag of peace.
Eef so be da Irish race
Ees da boss for all dees place,
Mak' dem be so great an' good,

Strong for granda brotherhood
    An' for peace.
Dey weell halp me, too, be gay
On your gladda feasta day,
    San Patrice!

AN INTERPAROCHIAL AFFAIR

OCH! there's divil a parish at all
    Like this one o' St. Paul.
Here the winter begins wid the fall
An' it sticks to the middle o' May.
Streets an' houses an' people are gray,
An' the night lends its hue to the day;
For the blessed sun's light hangs like fog on
    the walls
Where a man does be livin' his lone in St.
    Paul's.

Faith, 'tis odd that the same parish plan
Gave so much to St. Ann.
There's one parish that's fit for a man
Wid a hunger for warmth an' for light!
'Tis a comfort to find, day an' night,
Streets an' houses an' people so bright;
For there's summer-warm hearts an' there's
    kind, open han's,
An' a girl wid a face like a rose, in St. Ann's.

In a parish just over the line,
Called St. John the Divine,
There's a cozy new cot, an' it's mine!
Oh! 'tis I will have throuble to hide
From my face all the joy an' the pride
That my heart will be feelin' inside,
When next Sunday at Mass they'll be readin'
    the banns
For meself o' St. Paul's and Herself o' St.
    Ann's.

THE ITALIAN WIND

I DO not like da ween' dat blows
   Along da ceety street.
Eet breengs a message to da nose
   Dat ees not always sweet.
An', too, eet brags, dees ceety ween',
   How reech som' peopla are—
Dat's w'en eet's drunk with gasolene
   From passin' motor-car.
Eet ees no wondra I am sad
   For hear eet blow like dat
An' speak of theengs I nevva had
   An' nevva gona gat.

So, here I'm sad; but mebbe so
   I weell be happy yat.
Dere ees een countra-place I know
   A farm dat I can gat.
An' soon as I can finda man
   Dat like dees ceety street
An' buy from me dees leetla stan',
   I gona jomp at eet.

Ah! den w'en I am plant da leek
   An' garlic dere, you see,
Dose countra ween's dey sure weell speak
   Italian to me!

L'UNIVERSALE NOTA

DEES earth, so solid to our feet,
    Ees ours dat walk about on eet;
Yet men of manny deef'rent land
    Speak manny deef'rent way,
An' I can only ondrastand
    W'at my own peopla say.

Da sea, dat ees all lands baytween,
Not wan race for eets own can ween;
Yet frands of mine an' your frands, too,
    Mak' sooch sad calling from da sea,
Dey speak wan langwadge now to you
    An' wan same tongue to me.

April 15, 1912.

THE VESTIBULE

EVERY mansion, every cot,
    Be it great or small,
Hath a room, a tiny spot,
    Seldom praised at all.
Bards have sung of "marble halls,"
"Banquet rooms" and "pictured walls,"
    And of "gardens cool."
Not to these our thoughts belong;
We would make a little song
    Of "The Vestibule."

Unromantic little place,
    Narrow, close and bare?
Not if we in fancy trace
    All that happens there:
Welcome to the honored guest,
Little lips to mother's pressed
    Ere they start for school,
Lingering lovers' last good-night—
Lots of room for Fancy's flight
    In the vestibule!

There shall Fancy contemplate
    Still a greater bliss:

When the good wife speeds her mate
   With a morning kiss.
He who will not, when he may,
With this blessing start the day,
   Is a knave or fool.
Many cares are overthrown,
Many battles fought and won
   From the vestibule!

ROSA'S PARRAKEETS

ROSA, weeth her parrakeets,
    Tal da fortune een da streets.
Geeve her fiva cent an' see
W'at your fortune gona be.
Leetla birds so smart, so wise,
Seet een cage an' weenk deir eyes;
Seettin' een a row dey wait
Teell she ope' da leetla gate,
An' she tak' wan on a steeck,
Keessa heem an' mak' heem peeck
Fortune card out weeth hees beak.
W'at da card ees say to you
Mebbe so ees gon' com' true.
Som' day, mebbe, I weell see
W'at my fortune gona be.
Eef I could be parrakeet
Dat she eesa keess so sweet,
I am sure I would be wise
Jus' for lookin' een her eyes;

Mebbe so I be so smart
I find fortune een her heart!
Dat's a kinda fortune, too,
I could weesh ees gon' com' true.

DA SPREENG-CHARMER

"OH! ees eet true—you tal me so—
　　Da spreeng would com' eef you
　　　would go
An' play for eet?" say leetla Joe.

Den bigga Joe, da music-man,
He pat da leetla skeenny han'
An' "sure!" he say; "I go nex' week.
You see, my street-pian' ees seeck,
So lika you.　All weentra long
Eet was too cold for maka song;
But now I theenk a leetla beet
Your mediceene gon' feexin' eet?"
Joe smile, an' so da leetla boy
Smile, too, an' clap hees han's for joy;
An' all dat week he count da day
Teell time hees Pop shall go an' play.
So com' da day at las', an' dough
Steell een da streets ees ice an' snow,
Beeg Joe mus' do dees theeng for pleass
Dat leetla boy, aldough he freeze.

MADRIGALI

Den home agen dat night he say:
"I ain't quite do da treeck to-day;
You see, da spreeng mus' *hear* me play,
An' here een ogly ceety street
I no gat verra close to eet;
I musta go more far away."
So passa mebbe two, three day
An' notheeng com'. Wan night, bimeby,
Da leetla boy baygeen to cry,
So Joe say: "Wait a leetla beet
An' sure I weell be catchin' eet."
Nex' night he com' an' cry: "Hallo!
Here's granda news for leetla Joe.
To-day—O! verra, verra close—
I see da spreeng! An' w'at you s'pose?
Eet's justa leetla laughin' breeze
Dat jomp about among da trees!
An', O! eet dance so bright an' gay
So soon as eet ees hear me play;
I sure I catch eet soon som' day."

Bimeby, wan night, w'en Joe gat home,
He wheespra: "Sh! da spreeng ees com'!
Don't maka noise or you weell scare;
Eet's een da alley downa-stair!

You see, to-day w'en I am play
Out een da countra, far away,
Agen ees com' dat leetla breeze.
Eet keess da buds upon da trees,
An' tease da brook an' hop around
An' coax da flowers from da ground.
An' pretta soon so close I gat
I see eet keess a violat.
Den—presto! eet ees een my hat!
So here, O! leetla Joe, I breeng
For you, for you, da gladda spreeng!
'Sh! keepa steell, or you weell scare;
Eet's een da alley downa-stair."
"O! pleass," ees say da leetla boy,
An' he ees clap hees han's for joy,
"O! lat eet com' an' play weeth me."
Beeg Joe say: "No, not yat. You see,
To breeng eenside would nevva do;
Dat mak' eet seeck, more seeck dan you.
But, leetla Joe, you geeve eet time
An' pretta soon dat breeze weell climb
Outside upon your weendow-seell,
Eef you be good an' keepa steell."

Wan morna soon w'en Joe gat up
Da worl' ees lika wina-cup,

So reech an' sweet da air. An' so
He run an' cry to leetla Joe:
"Da spreeng! See now da leetla breeze
Ees at your weendow? Here eet ees!"
So den he leeft da window wide
An' lat da warma breeze eenside.
Da leetla boy he ope' hees mout'
An' breathe eet een an' breathe eet out,
An' laugh to feel eet een hees hair,
On han's an' face an' evrawhere.
"O! my, how sweet!" say bigga Joe.
"Com', sneeff eet een your nosa—so!—
Dat smal ees steeckin' to eet yat
From where eet keess da violat.
Ah! leetla Joe, w'at weell you do
For me dat catch da spreeng for you?"

Oh, my! sooch keesses warm an' long!
Sooch huggin', too, so glad, so strong!
You nevva see a leetla boy
Dat ees so crazy-wild weeth joy.
"Aha! deed I no tal you so,
Dat spreeng would com' so soon you go
An' play for eet?" say leetla Joe.

GIRLS WILL CHANGE

THEY say the girls they're raisin' here
    Has very takin' ways.
Mayhap 'tis true, but, dear, O! dear,
    'Tis not their likes I'd praise.
There's not a wan of all the lot
    I've ever chanced to see—
Not wan o' them—that ever got
    A heart-throb out o' me.
An', sure, I'm not so hard to pl'ase;
    'Tis I that used to know
A score o' maids deservin' praise—
    But that was long ago.

Although the times an' styles may change,
    A maid is still a maid;
But here she looks an' acts so strange,
    She's different, I'm afraid.
Mayhap the climate here's to blame
    For all the faults I see;
At anny rate, they're not the same
    As maidens used to be.

But Irish maids! Och, over there
  The girls I used to know
Were always sweet an' true an' fair—
  Was that so long ago?

W'EN SPREENG EES COM'

OH! 'scusa, lady, 'scusa, pleass',
    For dat I stop an' stare;
I no can halpa do like dees
    W'en Spreeng ees een da air.

I s'pose you know how moocha joy
Ees feell da heart of leetla boy,
W'en beeg parade ees passa by,
Eef he can climb da pole so high;
Or find on window-seell a seat
Where he can see da whola street,
An' watch da soldiers marcha 'way
An' hear da sweeta music play.
Ah! lady, eef dees joy you know,
You would no frown upon me so.
For, like da boy dat climb da pole,
From deep eensida me my soul—
My hongry, starva soul—ees rise
Onteell eet looka from my eyes
At all dat com' so sweet an' fair
W'en now da Spreeng ees een da air;
At greena grass, at buddin' trees
Dat wave deir branches een da breeze,

At leetla birds dat hop an' seeng
Baycause dey are so glad for Spreeng—
An' you dat look so pure, so sweet,
O! lady, *you* are part of eet!

So, 'scusa, lady, 'scusa, pleass',
    For dat I stop an' stare;
I no can halpa do like dees
    W'en Spreeng ees een da air.

APRIL'S WIZARDRY

I WOKE at dawn and heard the rain
    And far-off snarls of thunder.
I closed my eyes that sleep again
    Might draw my senses under;
And soon, in poppied warmth enfurled,
    I lost in sweet forgetting
The clamors of the stirring world,
    Its labors and its fretting.
        As from the bud
        The chill-checked flood
Of sap goes backward creeping,
        So falls this sense
        Of indolence
When April skies are weeping.

I woke in sunlight and arose.
    The joyful birds were chanting;
A young girl in the neighboring close
    Was busy at her planting.
I knew, as something erst unknown,
    The blessed charm of labor;
I loved—ah! not myself alone—
    I yearned to love my neighbor.

    As from the trees
    The sun and breeze
Their young leaves are beguiling,
    So from the heart
    Doth new life start
When April skies are smiling.

THE FALLEN TREE

THERE was a tree in Wister Wood
    Last April's livery wore
Of emerald leaf and crimson bud,
    But it is there no more.

There, earliest, on twig and bough,
    I marked the spring's advance;
Of all who note its absence now
    I only care, perchance.

Yet 'tis enough. For ne'er, for me,
    Shall any spring come in
But all its trees shall lovelier be
    Because this one hath been.

So may it be with me, whose blood
    Stirs ever when the spring
Calls out to me from Wister Wood
    And bids me rise and sing.

Enough for me, if when I've gone
    The way of man and tree,
Some spring be made more sweet for one,
    Through kindly thought of me.

DA FAITH OF AUNTA ROSA

YOU know my Aunta Rosa? No?
    I weesha dat you could;
She w'at you call "da leevin' saint,"
    Baycause she ees so good.
She got so greata, stronga faith,
    She don'ta nevva care
For doin' anytheeng at all
    But justa say her prayer.
She justa pray, an' pray, an' pray,
    An' work so hard at dat,
You theenk she would be gattin' theen
    Eenstead for gat so fat.
O! my, she gat so verra fat,
    Da doctor ees so scare',
He com' wan day to her an' say:
    "You mak' too moocha prayer;
Ees better do som' udder work
    An' tak' som' exercise."
My Aunta Rosa shak' her head
    An' justa leeft her eyes,
An' say: "I gotta faith so strong
    Dat I weell jus' baygeen

For pray dat I may lose da fat,
    An' soon I weell be theen."
So den she justa seet an' pray,
    So greata faith she feel,
An' nevva stop for anytheeng—
    Excep' for taka meal.
An' som' time, too, she seet an' mak'
    Da noise so loud an' deep;
Eet sounda verra mooch as eef
    She prayin' een her sleep.
So Aunta Rosa pray an' pray,
    But steell she gat more fat,
So fat she no can walk at all—
    Now, w'at you theenka dat?

Mus' be som' troubla een da sky;
    Mus' be ees som'theeng wrong!
Baycause eef Aunta Rosa got
    Da faith so great an' strong,
An' pray so hard dat eet ees all
    She gatta time to do,
I like som'body tal me why
    Her prayer ees no com' true!

WAITING FOR THE TRAIN

THE wood beyond the station thrills
    With glamor of the May;
The thrush his matin music trills,
   A-swing upon his spray,
And many things of beauty smile
   . And call me out to play,
Crying: "Tarry, O! tarry,
   For this one day."
      But Duty hath no pity!
      I am doomed to the city,
     And I hear the snorting demon that will
       carry me away.

How slowly plods the little boy
   Upon the road to school.
He yearns to taste a truant joy
   Where woodland depths are cool.
He lifts his guilty eyes to mine;
   I bid him run and play!
Crying: "Hookey! Play hookey,
   For this one day!"

But, O! for me the pity!
I am doomed to the city,
And I hear the snorting demon that will carry me away.

PADRE'S PEENCHA SNUFF

WHERE ees troubla—som' wan dead,
    Som' wan verra seeck een bed—
Leetla Padre Angelo
He ees dere bayfore you know.
Beatsa—how you call?—"da deuce"
How he eesa gat da news.
He mus' smal eet een da air;
Annyway, you find heem dere.
An' da firsta theeng he do,
W'en he hear da story through,
"Povero!" he say—you know
    Dat'sa mean "eet's tough"—
Den da Padre Angelo
    Taka peencha snuff.

Leetla Padre's boxa snuff
Mus' be funny kinda stuff,
Som'theeng dat he ainta use
Only w'en dere's badda news.
Mosta time dat we are meet
He ain't nevva theenk of eet,
But so soon he's comin' where
Eesa troubla een da air,

An' he hear da tale of woe,
He ees grab da boxa—so—
Like he eesa feel he no
   Jus' can gat enough,
W'en da Padre Angelo
   Taka peencha snuff.

Den he gona cough like dees:
"Hock-pachoo!" an' den he sneeze.
Den he blow hees nose a while,
Shak' hees olda head an' smile,
Rub da water from hees eye,
Looka queer an' say: "O, my!
Nevva find dees snuff so strong;
Mus' be here ees som'theeng wrong."
So he shak' hees head an' den
He ees rub hees eye agen.
Som' time I am theenk, you know,
   Eet'sa justa bluff,
W'en da Padre Angelo
   Taka peencha snuff.

THE SCOUTS OF SPRING

THE child at the window turned away
    With a parting glance at the leaden skies,
  And the look in the depths of his wistful eyes
Was hopeless and dull as they.
So came the night down, cold and gray,
    When the hidden sun had set.   * * *

Cold as the ashes of yesterday
    The morning breaks, and yet—
The scouts of Spring were abroad in the night.
    I heard them riding the rain.
I knew the touch of their fingers light,
As they swerved aside in their airy flight
    And tapped at the window-pane.
They swarmed like bees in the outer gloom;
    I heard them whispering there,
And I sensed them momently in the room
When their breathing tinged with faint perfume

The slumber-heavy air.
So hither and yon they danced and leapt;
And over one pillow they softly crept
    And called to the wild,
      Young heart of the child,
        Till the little limbs stirred, and the thin
          lips smiled
And he laughed aloud as he slept.
But there came a change at the wane of the
      night,
    And down from the hill,
      Where they'd long lain still,
The winds of Winter rode forth in their
      might.
The Spring's outriders broke in flight,
    And up from the east rose the morning
      gray,
      Cold as the ashes of yesterday.

*   *   *   *   *   *   *   *

"Wake!" cried the child beside my bed.
"Come to the beechwood, Sleepyhead!
    Wonders await you there. See here,
    Snowdrops! sweetest and first of the year;
Wake! for the Spring is come," he said.
Gray is the morning, gray and cold;

Ah! but the depths of his shining eyes,
Blue as the heart of the violet, hold
Joy and the glory of summer skies,
And their secrets manifold.

A SONG OF 'TONIO

EET was an Irish Maggie
    Dat catch my hearta first,
An' mak' eet jomp eensida me
    So like eet gona burst.
Dough een my breast was seengin' birds,
    My domba tongue was steell,
Baycause I had not Anglaice words
    For tal her how I feel;
She's gon', for dat I had not words
    For tal her how I feel.

Now com's Italian Rosa
    For mak' me love her more.
Da leetla birds eensida me
    Seeng louder dan bayfore.
But, O! I am so sadda man!
    My domba tongue ees steel;
I have no words Italian
    For tal her how I feel;
Not even words Italian
    For tal her how I feel.

THE WANDERING MIN-
STREL

OH! ye wealthy folk, blessed with a
　　heaped-over measure
　Of bodily comforts, of treasure and gold,
If your souls have been stirred for one
　　moment with pleasure
　By the catches I've sung or the jests I have
　　told,
　　　O! I pray ye, take heed of
　　　What most I'm in need of
　And loosen the strings of the purses ye
　　hold.
　　　Give the best that ye have
　　　For the best that I gave.
For the gay Merry-Andrew you've seen me
　　to-day
O! remember me, pray,
　　　　With your gold.

O! ye poor of God, blessed with warm
　　hearts ever throbbing
　With love for a fellow-man burdened with
　　cares,

If ye sense the soul-hunger, the sorrowful
    sobbing,
  In his merriest jests, in his liveliest airs,
    Ye will know and take heed of
     What most he's in need of,
  Both here and hereafter, wherever he
    fares.
    For the sorrow he's known
    That is like to your own,
When with tears of sweet pity your lashes
    are dim,
Have remembrance of him
      In your prayers.

PARADISE REGAINED

I'M a thing they call a "stevydore"—
　　Though some has called me worse—
An' I'm slavin' here along the shore
　　To fill a skinny purse;
For it's little that the wages are,
　　For all the counthry's free,
An' my hopes o' fortune still are far
　　As heaven is from me.
Still, though far away it seems,
There's a heaven in me dreams—
　　Blessid paradise I had an' lost, but hope
　　　　again to win—
An' it calls me from the breeze
That blows in acrost the seas
　　Whin a ship comes in.

"Sure, it's hell to be a stevydore,"
　　The lads beside me say;
But it's purgatory an' no more,
　　Since some may win away.
An' it's not forever that I'll slave
　　Within a stuffy hold,

For the pennies that I make an' save
   Will turn at last to gold.
O! the heaven that I knew,
Risin' green above the blue—
   Blessid paradise I had an' lost an'
     dreamed so much about—
'Tis mesel' wid joy will see
On a day that's soon to be
   Whin a ship goes out.

APRIL

APRIL,
    Irish through and through,
Here's my caubeen off to you!
Look you! now my head is bare,
Drop your tears upon my hair.
Weep your fill upon me, then
Warm me with your sun again.
Here's my heart. O! make its strings
Populous with linnets' wings.
So your holy birds are there
Not a ha'porth do I care;
Mute with sorrow, wild with glee,
So they make their home in me.

   April,
Dead, forgotten days
Tremble in your dim blue haze;
All the glories of the race
Flicker on your mobile face.
Heroes panoplied for fight
Glimmer in your golden light;

Martyrs, sanctified by pain,
Murmur in your silver rain.
All your smiles and all your tears
Voicing now our hopes and fears,
April, Irish through and through,
Here's my caubeen off to you!

EASTER EVE

A WORLD of sodden leaves and gaunt-
limbed trees
   That stand as in a dream. Set in the skies
   The moon, like embers of a watch-fire, lies
Half-quenched by mists breathed up from
restless seas;
And like a lion troubled in its sleep,
   The wind, high-cradled in the piney hills,
   By fits and starts with fretful moaning
thrills
The echoing air, and darkness rules the
steep.

And yet I know the sun will soon have kist
   With lip of fire the sky, so leaden-browed
Behind the silvern gossamer of mist.
   I know the Easter sun that gilds the cloud
   Shall kiss God's robes where last it
touched His shroud,
And all my soul is eloquent of Christ.

THE TEMPERAMENTAL
TOMMASSO

TOMMASSO can have, eef he want,
"Arteestica temperamant,"
But me, I am gladda for steeck
To workin' weeth shovel an' peeck.

You nevva can tal
Verra wal
Jus' w'en eet ees gona bust out—
Dees theeng dat I'm talkin' about.
Dees fallow Tommasso Barratt'
He nevva have notheeng like dat
Een all da long tima w'en he
Ees deeg een da streeta weeth me.
But all for a sudden wan day
He throw down hees shovel an' say:
"I gona be music-arteest!
Too moocha good time I have meessed,
An' so I gon' start righta 'way.
I jus' can'ta halp eet. I must,
Or som'theeng eenside me weell bust!"

An' so he ees study da art;
But now dat he's ready for start—
To-morrow, you see, ees da day
He's gona baygeen for to play—
Eet don't mak' heem happy wan beet.
He no can be steell een hees seat,
But tweest alla 'round een hees chair
An' pull hees mustache an' hees hair.
I say to heem: "Don'ta be scare';
Keep coola!" He tal me: "I can't!
Arteestica temperamant
Eensida me mak' me excite'
For fear I no playa jus' right."
I bat he no sleep mooch to-night.
I no like hees shoes on *my* feet!
He mebbe weell faint on da street
To-morrow, baycause he's excite'
An' sure won'ta do da theeng right.
You see, dees new musica-man
He don't verra wal ondrastan'
Da ways of da streeta-pian'.

Tommasso can have, eef he want,
"Arteestica temperamant,"
But me, I am gladda for steeck
To workin' weeth shovel an' peeck.

THE BUTT O' THE LOAFERS

OH! they needn't be so sly,
    All them lads when I pass by,
Wid their winkin' o' the eye
   An' their jokin' an' all that.
Sure, I'm wise enough to see
That the cause of all their glee
Is the ancient cut o' me
   An' me ould high hat.

Yerra! boys will have their play,
So I've not a word to say—
'Tis mesel' that wanst was gay
   As the gayest wan o' you;
An' there wasn't manny men
That'd care to joke me then,
When me blood was warm an' when
   This ould hat was new.

It was wid me an' me bride
When the blessid knot was tied,
An' it follied, when she died,
   Where they soon will lay me, too.

It has served me all these years,
Shared me pleasures and me tears—
As it's sharin' now the jeers
   O' the likes o' you!

Now, ould hat, we're worn an' sick,
But 'tis joy to think, avic,
That you never held a brick—
   An' there's some that can't say that!
So they needn't be so sly
Wid their winkin' o' the eye
When they see us passin' by,
   You an' me, ould hat!

A BALLADE OF BRIDES

FOR brides who grace these passing days,
    The poets lyric garlands twine;
For them the twittering song of praise
    Resounds with many a fulsome line.
    And unproved worth, as half divine,
Is glorified in tinkling tunes.
    But worthier dames shall bless our wine—
We'll toast the brides of other Junes!

What though a thoughtless public pays
    Its homage at young Beauty's shrine,
And wreathes smooth brows with orange sprays,
    With roses and with eglantine,
    Youth's cheeks that glow and eyes that shine
Are not the most enduring boons.
    O! we who've seen such things decline,
We'll toast the brides of other Junes!

Though flowery wreaths and poets' lays
    To grace the new-made bride combine,
O! let us rather twine the bays

For tried and true ones, thine and mine,
  Who share whate'er the fates design
To bless or blight our nights and noons;
  Good comrades still through rain or shine—
We'll toast the brides of other Junes!

L'ENVOI

Old Friend! whose bride of Auld Lang Syne
  Still fills thy life with honeymoons,
Thy glass to mine, my glass to thine—
  We'll toast the brides of other Junes!

DA GREATA BASABALL

OH! greata game ees basaball
    For yo'nga 'Merican.
But, O! my frand, ees not at all
    Da theeng for Dagoman.

O! lees'en, pleass', I tal to you
    About wan game we play
W'en grass ees green, an' sky ees blue
    An' eet ees holiday.
Spagatti say: "We taka treep
    For play da ball, an' see
Wheech side ees ween da champasheep
    For Leetla Eetaly."
So off for Polo Groun' we go
    Weeth basaball an' bat,
An' start da greata game, but, O!
    Eet ees no feenish yat!
Spolatro ees da boss for side
    Dat wait for catch da ball;
Spagatti nine ees first dat tried
    For knock eet over wall.
An so Spagatti com' for bat.
    Aha! da greata man!

Da han's he got; so beeg, so fat,
  Ees like two bonch banan'.
Spolatro peetch da ball, an' dere
  Spagatti's bat ees sweeng,
An' queeck da ball up een da air
  Ees fly like annytheeng.
You know een deesa game ees man
  Dat's call da "lafta-fiel'."
Wal, dees wan keep peanutta-stan'
  An' like for seettin' steell.
An' dough dees ball Spagatti heet
  Ees passa by hees way,
He don'ta care a leetla beet
  Eef eet ees gon' all day.
Da "centra-fielda man"—you know
  Dat's nex' to heem—he call:
"Hi! why you don'ta jompa, Joe,
  An' run an' gat da ball?"
But Joe he justa seetta steell
  Teell ball ees outa sight.
Dees mak' so mad da centra-fiel'
  He ees baygeen to fight.
Den com'sa nudder man—you see,
  I don'ta know hees name,

Or how you call dees man, but he
    Ees beeg man een da game.
He ees da man dat mak' da rule
    For play da gama right,
An' so he go for dose two fool
    Out een da fiel' dat fight.
He push da centra-fielda 'way—
    An' soocha names he call!—
An' den he grabba Joe an' say:
    "Com', run an' gat da ball."
But Joe he growl an' tal heem: "No,
    Ees not for me at all.
Spagatti heet da ball, an' so
    Spagatti gat da ball!"

O! greata game ees basaball
    For yo'nga 'Merican.
But, O! my frand, ees not at all
    Da theeng for Dagoman.

THE MAN'S THE MAN

"THE man's the man!" my Barney
     says—
   An' Barney's newly married—
"He's the wan that knows the ways
   The burdens should be carried.
Let the woman wear the grace
   An' pleasin' pranks o' beauty,
Yet be mindful of her place
   An' of her wifely duty;
By the crown within my hat,
   The chief of all our riches,
I'll be king o' this an' that;
   An' sure I'll wear the breeches;
Yes, an' need be, I can teach
   The 'Spanish way' o' walkin'!"
There's my Barney's manful speech—
   I listen to him talkin'.

"The man's the man!" my Barney says,
   An', faith, my thoughts are carried
Back to well-remembered days
   When I was newly married;

An' there's wan that's lookin' down
　　Upon this house this minute,
Knows who was it wore the crown
　　The whiles herself was in it.
Dull I was, but plain as day
　　'Tis now I'm seein' through it
How she let me have *her* way,
　　An' sure I never knew it;
Puffed wid pride as I could be
　　An' struttin' 'round an' squawkin',
"Man's the man!" sez I, an' she—
　　She listened to me talkin'.

DA SUMMER'S COM'!

OH! my, I'm glad da summer's com'
    An' school-books ees put by;
I do not like for show how domb
    Een evratheeng am I.

Me go to school? I guessa not!
But den you see, signor, I got
Wan leetla son of mine dat go—
Ah! smarta keed, Antonio!
He mak' me proud, he ees so queeck;
But som' time, too, eet mak' me seeck
Weeth—how you call eet now?—weeth
    shame
For dat I no can write my name.

But I, too, I am smarta 'nough
For looka wise an' maka bluff,
An' so he ainta catch me yat;
But he's so smarta keed, you bat
He's gona see som' day bimeby
How domb een evratheeng am I.
I tal you w'at eet's pretta tough
For always have to maka bluff,

To seet an' smoke an' be so near
At night-time, w'en he eesa here
Weeth all hees school-books, an' to fear
Dat he weell ask som' theeng or two
Dat gona mak' a fool of you.

W'at would you say—I ask you, pleass—
To soocha question lika dees
Dat jus' bayfore hees schoola stop
He aska me: "Hey! tal me, Pop,
W'en was eet came you Dagomans
Deescoverin' us 'Mericans?"

O! my, I'm glad da summer's com'
 An' school-books ees put by;
I do not like for show how domb
 Een evratheeng am I.

DA THIEF

EEF poor man goes
    An' stealsa rose
        Een Juna-time—
    Wan leetla rose—
You gon' su'pose
        Dat dat'sa crime?

Eh! w'at? Den taka look at me,
For here bayfore your eyes you see
Wan thief dat ees so glad an' proud
He gona brag of eet out loud!
So moocha good I do, an' feel,
From dat wan leetla rose I steal,
Dat eef I gon' to jail to-day
Dey no could tak' my joy away.
So, lees'en! here ees how eet com':
Las' night w'en I am walkin' home
From work een hotta ceety street,
Ees sudden com' a smal so sweet
Eet maka heaven een my nose—

I look an' dere I see da rose!
Not wan, but manny, fine an' tall,
Dat peep at me above da wall.
So, too, I close my eyes an' find
Anudder peecture een my mind;
I see a house dat's small an' hot
Where manny pretta theengs ees not,
Where leetla woman, good an' true,
Ees work so hard da whole day through,
She's too wore out, w'en com's da night,
For smile an' mak' da housa bright.

But, presto! now I'm home an' she
Ees seettin' on da step weeth me.
Bambino, sleepin' on her breast,
Ees nevva know more sweeta rest,
An' nevva was sooch glad su'prise
Like now ees shina from her eyes;
An' all baycause to-night she wear
Wan leetla rose stuck een her hair.
She ees so please'! Eet mak' me feel
I shoulda sooner learned to steal!

Eef "thief's" my name
I feel no shame;
　Eet ees no crime—
Dat rose I got.
Eh! w'at? O! not
　Een Juna-time!

WHAT THE FLAG SINGS

MY People! ye who honor me,
    Upon this day that made ye free,
And for your badge of liberty
    On high have set me,
Hear what my breeze-tossed ripples say,
Ere with the passing of this day
I once again am put away
    And ye forget me:

"In war begot, by war imbrued
Baptismally with patriot blood,
Triumphant, steadfast still, through good
    And evil omen,
I've watched victorious Peace alight
Upon the arms of Truth and Right,
Which nevermore shall fear the might
    Of foreign foemen.

"But, O! my people, help me preach
Our gospel now, that we may teach
Newcomers here of alien speech
    To know and love me.
Teach that the cause for which I stand,

The liberty of this fair land,
Will tolerate no Anarch brand
    To float above me.

"Aye! our own native faults lay bare!
Point out the specious statesman's snare,
Whose tongue would hide with shout and
    prayer
    His heart's sedition;
Who lifts to me his crafty eyes
And breathes abroad his soulful sighs,
Which not from love of me arise,
    But low ambition.

"O! teach and learn! And when the sky
This day's departing sunbeams dye,
And from the staff whereon I fly
    At last ye take me,
Remember what ye owe to me;
I'm but your *badge* of liberty,
And I no greater thing can be
    Than your deeds make me!"

July 4, 1912.

BALLADE OF SUMMER'S PASSING

LIKE a matron grown jaded—
   Fat, forty and fair—
In a nook cool and shaded,
   Who nods in her chair;
   Then, sudden, aware
Of the eyes of the masses,
   Feigns a wide-awake air,
Summer smiles as she passes.

All the charms she paraded
   In Junetime so rare,
When new roses were braided
   And twined in her hair,
   No longer are there.
All her gold but worn brass is,
   But, still debonair,
Summer smiles as she passes.

That her beauty is faded
   Beyond all repair,
All the pools where she waded—
   Her mirrors—declare.

    Brown limbs that are bare
Every woodland pool glasses;
    But what does she care?
Summer smiles as she passes.

ENVOY

Come, then, Autumn! and dare
    To be brave as this lass is,
When the like fate you share—
    Summer smiles as she passes.

SANCTUARY

HERE where ees my beez'ness place
   You can com' so mooch you pleass,
Call me "Dago" to my face,
   Joke weeth me an' sneer an' teass.
You can say my fruit ees bad,
   Growla 'bout da prices, too,
But I no can gatta mad;
   I mus' be polite weeth you.
Streeta keeds so small, so tough,
   Steala theengs an' run so queeck,
Here can treata me so rough
   Eet ees almos' mak' me seeck.
But I know where ees a door
   Feexa weeth a lock an' key;
Notheeng bother me no more
   W'en at night eet close on me.

O! so happy, happy door!
   I su'pose you got wan, too,
More for styleeshness an' more
   Fine an' gran' eet ees for you.
But w'en I seet down at night,
   All bust up from work all day,

All dat maka me excite'
　　Seem so verra far away,
I can mak' mysal' baylieve
　　I am good as anny man.
Notheeng den can mak' me grieve
　　Like at dees peanutta-stan'.
Peace ees com' eenside my door;
　　Push eet shut an' turn de key,
An' I am a man once more
　　W'en at night eet close on me.

SHAWN BHUI O'CONNOR

FROM the glens an' airy peaks
    Of McGillicuddy's Reeks,
        Shawn Bhui O'Connor
Draws the raw delights o' life.
Snare an' gun an' huntin'-knife
Are his all, for ne'er a wife
        Wears his name upon her.
Just his native hills alone
An' his wild sweet will can own
        Shawn Bhui O'Connor.

Save for powder an' for shot,
Village streets would know him not—
        Shawn Bhui O'Connor.
But the priest o' Ballymore
Often finds beside his door
Tribute for his frugal store,
        Knowing well the donor;
An' for gift o' grouse an' hare
Oft repays with kindly prayer
        Shawn Bhui O'Connor.

Mighty hunter, yet a child,
Shaggy nurslin' o' the wild—
    Shawn Bhui O'Connor.
Relic o' the primal man
Ere the Saxon race began;
Erin's lord an' sacristan
    Of her virgin honor,
May the peace o' God's free **air**
Keep you ever in its care,
    Shawn Bhui O'Connor!

Shawn Bhui—*Yellow John.*

AN ITALIAN LESSON

EEF you would be, O! 'Merican,
    Wise Dagoman like me
An' call een good Italian
    Da names for theengs you see,
Com', lees'en! an' I tal you true
How easy theeng eet ees to do.
    For firsta lesson, now, su'pose
        We taka som'theeng sweet;
    Dere eesa flower you calla "rose,"
        But w'at's my name for eet?
I mak' eet verra plain to you,
For here ees all you gotta do:

Say "Angela!" jus' "Angela!"
    An' eef you catcha sight
Of pretta face an' shinin' eyes
Dat smila like Italia's skies,
You bat my life you weell be wise
    An' justa wheesper "Angela!"
    An' sure you weell be right.

Eef you would know Italian
    For sweeta theengs you hear,

Here's wise Italian teacher-man
  Dat mak' eet plain an' clear.
Com', lees'en! an' I tal you true
How easy theeng eet ees to do.
    Dere eesa bird dat seeng so sweet—
      No sweeter song could be.
    "Thrush" ees da word you say for eet?
      Dat's not da word for me.
    You like to know Italian word
    I speaka for dees songa-bird?

    Say "Angela!" jus' "Angela!"
      An' eef so be you might
Have happiness for standin' near
W'en sounds wan voice so sweet an' clear
You theenk eet ees a thrush you hear,
    Say "Angela!" jus' "Angela!"
      An' sure you weell be right.

ARTFUL YOUNG BARNEY KEHOE

WILL ye be for the Gap o' Dunl e,
      I dunno?
O! I'm glad o' that same!
All the tourists think shame
To be missin' the Gap o' Dunloe—
      They do so.
Now, then, whishper! Mayhap,
When ye come on the Gap,
Ye'll be seein' a lass
On this side o' the pass
That'll ax for the toll.
She's a dacint good soul,
Though the eyes of her twinkle so droll.
Well, ye'll pay her the tax
An' ye'll wink an' ye'll ax:
"Would ye marry young Barney Kehoe?"—
'Tis a bit of a joke
That the folk love to poke
At the lass o' the Gap o' Dunloe.

An' it's where, whin ye've done wid Dunloe,
      Will ye go?

Ye'll be wise to come back
By this very same thrack,
Fur there's little that's back o' Dunloe—
    There is so.
Sure, the hills are so bare
There's no scenery there
Like the kind that ye find
On this side, d'ye mind?
So I'll watch for the day
Whin ye're passin' this way,
Jist to hear what the lass had to say,
Whin she made her reply
To the wink o' yer eye
An' yer joke at the Gap o' Dunloe—

Is it who may I be?
Ye'll find *me*, d'ye see,
If ye'll ax for young Barney Kehoe.

LEIGH WOODS NEAR BRISTOL TOWN

LEIGH Woods! and but a thought's
   flight from the ocean!
  Seemed time and space between
  As though they had not been;
As though a wave of mine own soul's
      emotion,
O'erwhelming my dazed senses in the smoke
And thunder of its cresting, here had broke
And cast me up beneath this English oak.
  Behind me lay the Avon-riven towns,
  Clouding with busy fires the autumn morning;
  But, O! the light of old romance adorning
   Leigh Woods and Durdham Downs!

An English wood! Not here, were mine the
      choosing,
  Would my foot first have trod
  The Old World's storied sod;
For here should rise ancestral wrongs,
      transfusing

Into my blood their heart-sepulchred teen.
Yet here were flow'ring fields and woods
    as green,
  Mayhap, as those wherein I would have
    been;
And leafy lanes as thronged with twinkling
    wings.
  The birds were singing here, not piping
    merely,
  Green-cloistered choirs intoning sweetly,
    clearly,
Of love, the crown of things.

Old passions melted in the holier fire
  Of Nature's motherhood;
  And o'er that English wood,
On finer air my soul soared high and higher.
  Trees, rocks, all senseless objects, great
    and small,
  All living things that walk or fly or
    crawl—
  Atoms of earth—I saw and loved them
    all!
Aye! rose I even to Heav'n's own parapet,
  On the strong wings of that unbridled
    rapture

Which, knowing once, I never shall re-
    capture—
But can no more forget.

O! could I catch again and hold forever
    The ecstasy, the power,
    Of that one fleeting hour,
Peace and the soul should never more
    dissever.
Forever through God's ether to be swirled,
And momently see Heaven's blue veils un-
    furled,
My song a silvern trumpet to the world!
    Leigh Woods! could I revive your spell
        again,
My soul would chant such music to the spirit,
The list'ning world, that could not choose
        but hear it,
    Would thrill as I did then.

Bristol, England, September 22, 1910.

CHATTERTON

"GRIM humorist!" I'd write upon his stone;
  "Great poet? Aye, but still a child of wit,
  And martyr to his judges' lack of it.
When first his mimic mintings rare were shown,
Befooled, they praised them, but, the fraud made known,
  They spurned his Rowley coinage, bit by bit.
  'No silver this,' they cried, 'but counterfeit!'
Not seeing it was gold and all his own.

"Oh! dear deceiver, child of mystery!
  How well to the last hour he played the game,
And falsely strong in his adversity,
  Hid his young honor in a cloud of shame.
And last, the play's meet epilogue we see:
  Death—but dissembled by undying fame!"

Bristol, England, September, 1910.

KERRY UNVISITED

FAIR was the sky and calm the sea,
   Aye, calmer than this bosom,
When first upon my vision broke
   The Skelligs, wild and gruesome.
As slow the rugged coast-line rose
   Above the sunlit ocean,
O! bitter was the fight I waged
   To still my heart's commotion.
Scion of exiles, home again!
   Each rock and tree and steeple
Encircled by my eager glass
   Brought greetings from my people.
My kindly shipmates little guessed—
   So gay I seemed and merry—
What tears were bubbling in my breast
   For the holy hills of Kerry.

So all day long I kept the deck,
   And fed my soul with gazing
On cliffs and bays and over all
   The hills their green crowns raising.
When through the dusk the ship sailed on
   And found her English haven,

At dawn, where Bristol Channel takes
  The waters of the Avon,
To me the Saxon tyrants came,
  But kindlier than the olden,
And loaded me with captive chains.
  Though here those chains were golden,
And royal hospitality
  Made every moment merry,
My heart was where my people lie
  Among the hills of Kerry!

* * * * * * * *

O! calm again were sea and sky.
  The good ship, homeward turning,
Bore with her one whose heart was sore
  With unrequited yearning.
Again I watched the Kerry coast,
  Behind our white wake falling;
The Sidhe were on those fading hills!
  I know; I heard them calling.
Then rose the answering sea in wrath,
  The sky grew gray above it,
The storm broke and the shuddering ship
  Quaked in the clutches of it.
And like the Ancient Mariner,
  Whose sin no seas could bury,
I knew what spirits shook our keel—
  The wild, wild Sidhe of Kerry!

Laugh not to scorn this tale of mine
  As some wild dreamer's notion;
I read reproach in every thing
  That tracked me o'er the ocean.
The angry sea that snatched at me,
  The winds at night that jeered me,
The very gull that screamed o'erhead
  And fled as though it feared me;
I was the plague upon the ship
  That made her groan and shiver
Through toil of seven days and nights
  To reach this peaceful river.
So now I swear: No more for me
  The ocean-girdling ferry;
No more for me, unless it be
  To tread the hills of Kerry!

SS. "Royal Edward," approaching Montreal, October 6, 1910

Sidhe (pronounced "Shee")—*the Fairies.*

MR. HAIL COLOMB'

IRISH, Anglaice, Dootchman, Jew,
   W'at'sa matter weetha you?
Why you no keep holiday,
Wave da flag an' shout "Hooray"?
Why you laugh an' weenk your eye
W'en da beeg parade go by?
Ain't you glad for anytheeng
W'en da leetla cheeldren seeng?
Lika me you oughta be
Glad for granda liberty
Dat you all are gattin' from
      Hail Colomb'.

Can eet be you are so domb
You don't know dees "Hail Colomb' "?
He ees Dago sailorman
Firsta find dees greata lan'.
Poor he was, but, O! rejoice,
Tak' your hat off, leeft your voice,
Maka prayer of thanks baycause
Dere's no Eemigration laws,
Dere's no Ellis Island w'en
Weeth hees ragged sailormen
First to deesa shores ees com'
      Hail Colomb'.

OCTOBER SONG IN ROMANY

MOTHER and wife to me,
    Fostering Earth!
Sum of all life to me,
    Birth to rebirth;
Mother, at urge of the sun-god who bore me,
Wife, whose cool bosom at last shall swell
    o'er me,
    Ever and ever my heart shall be thine.
Ah! but one season brings *thy* heart the
    nearest,
When to my loving thy bosom thou barest.
    Then thou art mine.

    Summer brings many men
      Singing thy praise,
    But are there any when
      Chill are the days?
Now, when thy robes are but tatters and
    patches,
Sport of the winds in the bitter night watches,
    Stronger and truer my heart beats to thine.

My breast to thine and the deep sky our
  cover,
Quiet and peace for the loved and the
  lover—
  Now thou art mine!

THE MAGIC APPLE

"A THING of beauty is a joy forever."
    Though years becloud it, never
        may they sever
Its lovely essence utterly from earth;
Never a joy was born but hath rebirth.
There was a sunset lost, long, long ago,
    An autumn sunset seen through orchard
        boughs.
A boy's eye brightening in the amber glow
    Gave to his mind no more of it to house
For the delight of manhood's pensive days
Than the bare memory of time and place;
      So nigh forgot, it seemed
      As something he had dreamed.
Yet now the man, before whose boyish ken
    The glory melted on the evening breeze,
Knows it lived on, for he hath found again
    His long-lost sunset of the orchard trees.

A penny tribute to a swarthy vendor
Hath filled for me this city street with
    splendor.
A meagre apple! yet its crushed pulp drips
A long-forgotten savor on my lips,

A rare, faint essence tasted once before,
  But only once; and suddenly I find
The honeyed gush hath loosed a long-locked door,
  And all the olden splendor floods my mind.
    A care-free lad I stand,
    An apple in my hand,
And watch the amber glory grow and wane.
  I feel upon my cheek the evening breeze.
Joy lives forever! I have found again
  My long-lost sunset of the orchard trees!

A SONG TO GIULIA

DERE ees a tree een Mad'son Square
    Dat stan' bayfore me now;
An' he ees old an' tweest' an' bare,
    Weeth holes een trunk an' bough.
He stan' so ogly an' alone,
    Dees good-for-notheeng tree,
He could be brother of my own,
    He ees so lika me.

See now dat tree een Mad'son Square
    W'en blows da weentra storm!
So manny leetla birds are dere
    Eenside hees heart so warm.
Now he ees proud, dat ogly tree,
    An' strong and happy, too.
Ah! so da heart eensida me
    Dat warm my thoughts of you!

THE TIDES OF LOVE

FLO was fond of Ebenezer—
   "Eb," for short, she called her beau.
Talk of tides of Love, great Caesar!
   You should see them—Eb and Flo.

WHEN DORANDO BEAT HAYES

YOU theenk eet strange for dat I am
So meek, so quiet lika lamb,
Eenstead for brag a leetla beet
About da greata granda feat
Of leetla Dagoman dat ran
An' beat so bad da Irishman?
Of course, signor, eet eesa true
I like to say a word or two.
But w'at'sa use? Een deesa lan'
Dere ees so manny Irishman
Dat ees so queeck for gat excite'
An' alla tima wanta fight,
I notta care for show da pride
An' joy my heart ees feel eenside.
Dorando ees so strong, so gran',
He need no be afraid for stan'
Een front of manny Irishman
An' brag a leetla beet, an' tal
How slow dey are; but I, mysal',
I no can run so verra wal.

THE ABSENT-MINDED SHE

SHE called me "Jack!" But instantly
   She blushed as red as red could be,
And bit her lip, as if to show
And she meant not to have spoken so;
All which I was not slow to see.

'Twas something of a shock to me;
I felt no very great degree
Of palpitating joy, although
   She called me "Jack."

It was, indeed, a mystery
Until I thought of John Supplee.
   Was *he* her "Jack," I'd like to know?
   You see, my given name is "Joe."
The absent-minded, fickle She—
   She called me "Jack!"

W'AT'S A "NORAYSUICIDE?"

IRISH Padre Tommeeckbride
  Laugh so mooch an' hold hees side,
I no mak' heem ondrastan',
Dough I talk so good's I can,
W'en to-day I go for see
Eef he pleassa marry me.
Den he call me soocha name
Eet ees maka me ashame'.

"Pleassa, Padre"—so I speak—
"I want marry nexta week."
"So?" he look at me an' say,
"You be bapatiza, eh?"
"No," I say, "you are meestak';
Weddin's w'at I want you mak'."
Steell how mooch I am esplain
I no gat eet een hees brain.
Alla time he justa cries:
"Where an' w'en you bapatize?"

Den my Rosa's brothra Joe—
He ees weetha me, you know,

An' ees smart as he can be—
He ees wheespera to me.
"Oh!" I say, for now ees plain
Mebbe so w'at Padre mean,
"First we want da weddin' here;
Bapatisma nexta year!"
Den da Padre laugh an' say:
"Noraysuicida, eh?"

Why you laugha? Dat'sa shame,
Callin' poor man soocha name!
Why ees Padre Tommeeckbride
Call me "Noraysuicide"?

DA NO-GOOD WORKAMAN

I AM ashame' weeth deesa man
   For dat he ees Italian,
  An' justa lazy slob;
We no could mak' good 'Merican
Of Joe Marelli from Milan—
  An' so he lose hees job.

Las' mont' w'en he ees landin' here,
He feel so strange an' look so queer,
I'm sad for heem as I can be
An' gat heem job for work weeth me
For deeg da tranch een deesa street.
At first he's verra glad for eet,
But steell eet ees no verra long
Bayfore he eesa gona wrong.
At evra stranja sight an' sound
He drop hees peeck an' looka 'round.
Eef mebbe so a sparrow hop
Near where he work eet mak' heem stop.
So, too, he watch eef on da street
Som' cheeldran com' weeth dancin' feet;
An' som'time w'en from far away
He hear da banda moosic play,

He stan' weeth head on wanna side
An' ears an' moutha open wide.
Wan time w'en breeze dat sweep da street
Breeng newsapaper to hees feet,
He tak' an' try for readin' eet!

But theeng dat tak' hees job away
Ees dees dat happen yestaday:
Som' lady drop from passin' car,
Right een da streeta where we are,
Beeg boncha flower dat's halfa dead,
But pretta, yallow, white an' red—
You know dees flower weeth bushy head?
Chreesanthew'at? Ah! yes, dat's eet—
Wal, Joe he see dem een da street
An' run an' grab dem uppa queeck,
An' den he tak' dem back an' steeck
Dem up on top da dirta pile,
An' lay dem out een soocha style
An' feex dem weeth so fina care,
You theenk for sure dey growin' dere!
An' pretta soon dey catch da eye
Of evra wan dat's passin' by.
Eh? Sure dey looka pretta so,
But seence eet ees no *work*, you know,
Da boss raise som'theeng alse for Joe!

So I am 'shame' weeth deesa man
For dat he ees Italian,
  An' soocha lazy slob;
We no could mak' good 'Merican
Of Joe Marelli from Milan—
  An' so he lose hees job.

OCH!

OCH! the year is gettin' gray,
    Like a man that's had his day,
Waitin', jisht, to fade away
    An' none to pity.
Och! the way the winds do blow!
Little ease o' them ye'll know,
Whether in the fields ye go
    Or in the city.

Och! how fasht the leaves do fall!
Reekin' fires an' smoky pall—
Och! 'tis like a funeral,
    So cold an' sober.
Och! the stillness ev'rywhere!
Och! there's witches in the air!
Och! the smell o' death that's there!
    Och! Och-tober!

THE GOLDEN GIRL

R ED hair!
    Isn't it quare?
Once on a time I'd do nothin' but jeer at it.
    Now, faith,
    Look at me teeth,
See how I show them an' growl when you
    sneer at it.

    Brown eyes?
    "Muddy wid lies,"
"Dull an' deceitful," I once was decidin'
    them;
    But—whack!—
    Yours will go black
Under me fist now, if you'd be deridin' them.

    What's more,
    Freckles galore
Made a complexion the worst I could deem
    of it;
    But now—
    You must allow
They give a touch o' pure gold to cream of it.

　　　　Some girls
　　　　Flaunt the red curls,
But it is blue eyes inundher that gaze at ye;
　　　　Some own
　　　　Freckles alone—
Let them be oglin' as much as they pl'ase
　　at ye.

　　　　One charm
　　　　Needn't alarm;
Fear not the lass who is only unfoldin' one;
　　　　But she
　　　　Blessed wid all three—
Like my own Nora—Och! *She* is the golden
　　one.

LABOR'S SABBATH

LET this, Labor's Sabbath-day,
  Be a day of pleasure.
Toll no bells and nothing play
  But a jolly measure.
Labor's very self is prayer,
  Serious and holy;
So its holiday should wear
  Naught of melancholy.

Sure, no temple walls should irk
  Labor's gala spirit,
Whose least sounds of daily work
  Soar to Heaven or near it.
We could build no fitting fane
  Dedicate to Labor,
Till the World shall learn again
  Love of God and neighbor;
As, of old, the pure of heart
  (You have heard the story)
Reared Cathedral walls at Chartres,
  Still its greatest glory.
Prince and peasant, belle and wench,
  Toiling in all weather,

Hauled the stone and dug the trench,
  Praising God together.
Those who set their hates aside
  Only were selected;
And who would not were denied
  And their gifts rejected.
Love endureth over art,
  Art is transitory,
But the twain combined at Chartres
  Blossomed into glory.
Till the World shall strive again
  Thus for God and neighbor,
We shall rear no fitting fane
  Dedicate to Labor.

So let Labor's Sabbath-day
  Be a day of pleasure.
Toll no bells and nothing play
  But a jolly measure.
Labor's very self is prayer,
  Serious and holy;
So its holiday should wear
  Naught of melancholy.

A CHILD'S CHRISTMAS SONG

LORD, I'm just a little boy,
    Born one day like You,
And I've got a mother dear
    And a birthday, too.
But my birthday comes in spring,
    When the days are long,
And the robin in the tree
    Wakens me with song.
Since the birds are all away,
    Lord, when You are born,
Let Your angels waken me
    On Your birthday morn.

Lord, I'm just a little boy,
    Hidden in the night;
Let Your angels spy me out
    Long before it's light.
I would be the first to wake
    And the first to raise
In this quiet house of ours
    Songs of love and praise.

You shall hear me first, dear Lord,
 Blow my Christmas horn;
Let Your angels waken me
 On Your birthday morn.

UNDER THE HOLLY

"THIS is not the mistletoe;
    It is merely holly.
You've no right to kiss me so;
This is not the mistletoe,
That has berries white as snow;
    These are red," said Molly.
"This is not the mistletoe,
    It is merely holly."

"This *must* be the mistletoe,
    Though it looks like holly,
Though the berry's red," said Joe,
"This must be the mistletoe.
Every berry's blushed to know
    'Twas not fair as Molly.
This must be the mistletoe,
    Though it looks like holly."

A CHRISTMAS CAROL

THERE was a Star whose light,
    Mystical and holy,
Shone through the quiet night
    O'er a stable lowly.
Sing praise to God on high!
    And rejoice that He
Thus should beatify
    Humble poverty.

A Merrie Christmas, Gentlefolk!
    And may your wealth and pride
Be mindful of the humble ones
    This blessed Christmastide.

There was a Little Child,
    Innocent and holy,
Born of the Virgin mild
    In that stable lowly.
Sing praise to God, who gave
    Unto you and me
Such Gift our souls to save!
    Oh! the Charity!

A Merrie Christmas, Gentlefolk!
  And may your wealth and pride
Be mindful of the humble ones
  This blessed Christmastide.

DA COLDA FEET

DA beggarman across da way
    Ees happy as can be;
He laugh an' weenk baycause he theenk
    He gotta joke on me.

O! my! O! my! how cold eet ees
    For stan' on deesa street!
Da weends blow like dey gona freeze
    Da shoes upon your feet.
I nevva see een deesa town
    So fierce da weentra storm;
I keepa hoppin' up an' down
    For mak' my feeta warm.
But beggarman across da way
    He stan' against da wall,
So like eet was a summer day;
    He ees no cold at all.
Ees justa box een fronta heem
    For hold hees teenna cup,
But he bayhava so eet seem
    A stove for warm heem up.
An' evra time he look an' see
    How colda man am I,

He justa weenk an' laugh at me
   So like he gona die!
An' so I leave dees fruita stan'
   An' walka 'cross da street
For see how ees dees beggarman
   Can keep so warma feet.
I look, an' dere I see da legs
   Dat prop heem by da wall
Ees notheeng more dan wooden pegs—
   He got no feet at all!

Eef colda feet should mak' you swear
   An' growl so bad as me,
I bat your life you would no care
   So mooch eef you could see
Da beggarman across da way,
   So happy as can be,
Dat laugh an' weenk baycause he theenk
   He gotta joke on me!

SONG OF THE CHRISTMAS TREE

ONCE out of midnight sweet with mystery
The wonder of all wonders came to be;
So shall the dawn a marvel make of me.
For when in all my beauty I am born
In the first glimmer of the Christmas morn,
Angels of innocence in mortal guise
Shall look upon me with their faith-big eyes;
      And, looking, see
      A greater thing in me
Than the bare figure of a tree.
      Behold! in every limb
      I thrill with praise of Him
For whom I stand in memory.

Kings of the East and wise men three there were
Who brought to Him rare frankincense and myrrh.
So do my balsamed branches when they stir
In the warm airs that move about this room,
And render forth their homage in perfume.

Lift up your hearts anew, O! care-worn
    men,
Look up with glad, believing eyes again;
       And, looking, see
        A greater thing in me
    Than the bare figure of a tree.
       Behold! in every limb
        I thrill with praise of Him
    For whom I stand in memory.

DA POLEETICA BOSS

GIUSEPPE Baratta ees great politeesh';
   He w'at you call "Dago poleetica boss."
He peeck da best man for da Pres'dant poseesh',
   An' show how you vote jus' by maka da cross.
He say: "Nevva minda w'at som'body tal
   W'at dees man or dat man ees goin' do for you.
You no ondrastan' deesa theeng verra wal,
   So jus' wait an' see w'at I tal you to do."

Giuseppe he study an' theenk an' he work
   So hard for deescovra w'eech side eesa best,
Ees nobody else een da ceety Noo York
   So theen like he gat an' so needa da rest.
Ees holes een hees shoe where da toes ees steeck through;
   Hees clo'es dey are look jus' so bad as dey can.

He say: "Eet ees harda for know w'at to
    do—
  I guess we weell vote for da Democrat
    man."

But steell he work hard for be sure he ees
    right,
  An' study som' more; an' so—presto!—
    wan day,
He com' weetha face ees so shiny an' bright,
  I see dat at las' he ees find da right way.
He gotta new shoes an' new pants an' new
    coat
  An' looka so styleesh an' fine as he can.
He say: "Ees meestak'! We gon' chanja
    dat vote.
  Ees besta for vote for Republica man."

Giuseppe Baratta ees great politeesh';
  Hees heart ees so true an' hees brain ees
    so bright,
He work an' he study, baycause he no weesh
  For mak' up hees mind teell he sure he
    ees right.

THOUGHTS OF ROSA

EEF only flow'rs dalight your eye
    An' museeck please your ear,
Baycause dey mak' you theenk an' sigh
    For her you lova dear,
Ees mebbe so da girl you trace
    Een soocha softa theeng,
Ees only pretta een da face
    Or gotta voice to seeng.
        But, O! da wife I gona gat
        She ees so fine an' strong an' fat!
        You nevva could su'posa
           How mooch I meet
           Een ceety street
        Dat mak' me theenk of Rosa.

I nevva see da horse so strong
    Dat pull an' worka so,
I nevva hear da louda song
    Dat steama-wheestles blow—
All theengs een deesa beezy worl'
    Dat nevva stop for rest—
Weethouta theenkin' of da girl
    Dat I am love da best.

For, O! da wife I gona gat
She ees so fine an' strong an' fat!
You nevva could su'posa
   How mooch I meet
   Een ceety street
Dat mak' me theenk of Rosa.

OULD MATT'EW MORAN

"OCH! 'tis he that looks natural, layin'
    there dead,"
  Said ould Matt'ew Moran,
"Wid the palms at his feet an' the lights at
    his head
  An' the cross in his han'.
    Heart an' soul are at rest,
    An' it's all for the best,"
  Said ould Matt'ew Moran.

When he'd laid by his coat an' had hung up
    his hat,
An' had shuffled away to a corner an' sat
Wid his stick twixt his knees an' his han's on
    the crook,
'Twas himsel', an' no less, had the "natural
    look."
For the folk o' the parish were wont to
    declare
Ne'er a wake a success unless Matt'ew was
    there.

" 'Tis a sorrowful world," he leaned over
    an' said
To the man by his side, wid a shake of his
    head;
"There's so much in it now that's deceitful
    an' wrong,
'Tis a blessin' our fri'nd here was took
    while he's young."
"He was siventy-five lasht July," said the
    man,
"An' I doubt if ye're more than that,
    Misther Moran."
Wid a tap o' the end of his stick on the floor,
"Sure, a man is as ould as he feels—an' no
    more!"
    Said ould Matt'ew Moran.

"Och! the breed o' men found in these days!
    'Tis a crime!
Sure, they're not the strong stuff that was
    raised in my time.
Who's the nixt wan to go? If ye'll jisht look
    around,

Ye'll find manny a sickly wan here, I'll be
    bound.
There's no life in thim now like the lads in
    my day."
So he sat in his chair an' jisht muttered away,
While the neighbors came in an' passed out
    o' the door
In a stiddy procession. Ten minyits or more
Since the ould man had spoken, the man by
    his side
Found him sittin', asleep, wid his mouth open
    wide.
Undisthurbed in his corner they let him
    dream on
Till the lasht o' the neighborly mourners
    was gone.
"I've been noddin'," sez he, as he rose to
    his feet;
"Och! the houses these days are jisht
    murthered wid heat,"
  Growled ould Matt'ew Moran.

"There's so much in the world that's deceit-
    ful an' wrong,"
  Said ould Matt'ew Moran,

" 'Tis a blessin' indeed to be took whin ye're
        young,
    Like that dacint young man.
        Well, there's wan gone to rest,
        An' it's all for the best,"
    Said ould Matt'ew Moran.

IL GRILLO

YOU like to go to Italy,
　　You weesh for veesit Roma?
All right, you com' an' seet weeth me
　　To-night w'en I am homa.
Dough mebbe so da weentra storm
　　Outside ees nevva quiet,
Da keetchen fire weell be warm
　　While we are seettin' by it;
An' eef so be you close your eyes
　　You easy can pretanda
You are beneath da sunny skies
　　Dat smile upon my landa.
An' pretta soon, so sweet, so clear,
　　W'en evratheeng ees steel, O!
W'at pretta song ees dees you hear?
　　Il grillo, O! il grillo!

　　Ha! nevva mind da snow,
　　An' how da weend ees blow:
　　　　"Hoo-woo! hoo-woo! hoo-wee!"
　　For here eet's warm, an', O!
　　Il grillo seenga so:
　　　　"Cher-ree! cher-ree! cher-ree!"

How com's he to dees colda clime
  To seeng so far from homa?
I catch heem manny, manny time
  W'en I am boy een Roma.
I catch heem een da fields an' tak'
  Heem back eento da ceety,
Where reecha peopla try to mak'
  Deir gardens fine an' pritty.
Dey are so glad for hear heem seeng
  Dey no can gat too manny,
An' so for evra wan I breeng
  Dey geeva me a penny.
Dough here hees song ees justa same,
  Hees name I no can speak eet—
Eh? w'at you call hees Anglaice name?
  Ah! "creecket," yes, "da creecket."

  'Sh! nevva mind da snow,
  An' how da weend ees blow:
    "Hoo-woo! hoo-woo! hoo-wee!"
  For here eet's warm, an', O!
  Il grillo seenga so:
    "Cher-ree! cher-ree! cher-ree!"

THE ONE THING LACKING

OH! my, signor, eet eesa true
    Dere's jus' wan theeng I envy you;
Eef I was *borna* 'Merican,
I sure would be da happy man.

You see, dere ees a girl I know
Dat's name' Bianca D'Angelo;
Italian, of course, but she
Com' verra yo'ng from Italy.
She's pretta girl an' verra bright,
An' she can speak an' read an' write
Dees Anglaice jus' so good as you;
An' alla time she's crazy, too,
For readin' books dat tal you of
All kinda peopla makin' love;
An' som'times I am workin' near
An' justa can'ta halp but hear.
Wal, w'en she's readin' so wan day,
She stop an' looka far away,
Den to da girl nex' door she say:
"Da man I gona love mus' be
Da handsomest I evva see.
He mus' be brave an' fulla fun,

Yat strong for maka playnta mon';
An' he mus' have good disposeesh'
An' geeve me evratheeng I weesh.
An' w'en dees pretta hero com'
For mak' me queen of all hees home,
All common peopla een da land
Mus' standa' 'round an' clap da hand
Baycause he ees so fine an' grand!
He mus' be all dese theengs—an' he
True borna 'Merican mus' be."

Eet's jus' dose last few word, you see,
Dat's spoilin' evratheeng for me!
Eef I was *borna* 'Merican,
I sure would be da happy man.

BUSINESS DIPLOMACY

EES fat Dootch barber gotta shop
   T'ree door from deesa bootblack stan',
An' w'en he see da trade I gat
  He try for bust me eef he can,
An' so he geeve outside hees shop
  A chair for neegger bootblack man.

You theenk dat I am feela bad
For see heem gat som' trade I had?
      Ah! no, my frand,
      I mak' pretand
To smile an' seeng, I am so glad.

Firs' theeng you know ees Meester Smeeth
  Dat use' for gat hees shine from me,
He stop for shine from neegger man.
  I mak' pretand I do not see,
But neegger man he mak' da face
  An' ees so glad as he can be.

You theenk dat I am feela bad
For see heem gat dees trade I had?
      Ah! no, my frand,
      I mak' pretand
To smile an' seeng, I am so glad.

Nex' day w'en comesa Meester Smeeth,
   I say, "Good-morna" justa same.
So jus' baycause I am polite
   Eet mak'sa Meester Smeeth ashame'.
So he com' back; so evra wan
   Ees com' back where dey always came!

Da neegger man ees gatta mad,
An' growl an' swear; he feel so bad.
        But I, my frand,
           I mak' pretand
I do not see—but I am glad.

AN IDYLL OF OLD JOYS

WHY shouldn't I speak of our exploit that morning out at the farm?
Undignified? What if it was, Judge? We didn't do any great harm;
And nobody saw us, that's certain, for the rest of the folks were asleep,
And—well—O! well, Judge, it's a story and really too good to keep.
Besides, you're to blame for it all, Judge, for you must admit it was you
Suggested the thing; and I'm certain I'd never have gone if you two,
Yes, you and your crony, the Colonel, hadn't tapped at my bedroom door,
Disturbing my peaceful slumber at the ridiculous hour of four.
The "best time to fish," you assured us, and hopefully led us away
Up over the hills that were faintly predicting the coming of day,
And so, to the lake in the hollow, green-rimmed by its deep-wooded shores,

And then, when we got in the boat, Judge,
　　with you hard at work with the oars,
We found you'd forgotten the bait—Eh?
　　What nonsense! Of course, it was you.
We brought your fault home at the time,
　　Judge, and made you acknowledge it,
　　too.
O! well, let it pass. Then the Colonel benignly remarked that although
Our fishing was off for that morning, we
　　ought to have something to show;
We shouldn't go home empty-handed, he
　　said, and suggested the joys
Of hunting those silly pond-lilies, like so
　　many Sunday school boys.
You fell into line with the notion and started
　　to row us in-shore,
And then we discovered that spring-board
　　we never had noticed before.
We gazed at the board and each other, and
　　gazed at the spring-board again;
You trailed one fat hand in the water and
　　twiddled your fingers—and then
You gave us the two-fingered signal that no
　　fellow ever forgets.

We looked and we grinned at each other and whispered in chorus: "Let's!"
There wasn't a soul there to see us, so we just beached the boat with a rush
And fell to discarding our garments in the leafy underbrush.
And I was first in—what? Nonsense! All right, we'll say you were the first,
But, say, Judge, your plunge from that spring-board was positively the worst.
I know; you just thought you'd be pretty and dove too high and too straight,
Fetched bottom, and came up snorting and rubbing your shiny pate.
I had to laugh so at the Colonel—Ungainly? Yes, wasn't he, though?
My dive? Well, it would have been graceful if you hadn't hurried me so.
But, say, when you ducked the poor Colonel, I thought that was shabby of you,
And you sixty-four last December and he only sixty-two!
It served you right, too, that you had to "chaw beef" when you started to dress.
What? Me? Why, I didn't do that, Judge; that trick was the Colonel's, I guess.

But wasn't it great, though? And didn't
    you thrill when your body shot in,
With nothing 'twixt you and the water, just
    nothing at all but your skin?
We'd come to this lake rather often and
    bathed in the full light of day,
With throngs of those summer sojourners
    who fritter their time in that way;
But then there were thick bathing garments
    to cumber us, body and limb,
And that sort of thing's but a "bath," Judge,
    but this was a regular "swim"!
And then, walking back to the farmhouse,
    with the rising sun in your face,
Just gilding the hilltops with glory, you
    thrilled with a newly-found grace
That wakened a host of sweet memories
    these long years forgotten, and then—
Say, Judge, if we go back next summer, I
    dare you to do it again!

FINER CLAY

SURE, I used to think a pipe was the
    glory of a man,
  Troth I did then, Mary Ann.
Long before my years were ripe (wid a
    rattle in one han')
  I would smoke one, Mary Ann.
An', thinks I, there's nothin' gives
To the grandest man that lives
Such a finish, ye may say;
An' it's well I mind the way
That it nearly finished me.
But I wouldn't let it be
  Till I liked it, Mary Ann.

Then I found an ould dhudeen was a comfort
    to a man,
  An' none betther, Mary Ann;
For wid that my teeth between, if I'd work
    to do or plan,
  It was aisy, Mary Ann.
An' the more I smoked my clay,
All the more I worked away;
An' my thoughts were keen an' long

When the pipe was goin' strong.
For the two of us, ye see,
Were just suited to a "t"
　Wid each other, Mary Ann.

So the pipe became my all, an' meself, a
　　　lonely man,
　Grew to love it, Mary Ann.
But there's changes do befall that ye never
　　　un'erstan';
　Faith, they do, then, Mary Ann.
An' to-night there's somethin' wrong;
For I've sat here thinkin' long,
But my thoughts an' pipe don't fit,
For I cannot keep it lit.
What I'm tellin' ye is true,
An' the throuble, dear, is *you*—
　Sure, it's jealous, Mary Ann!

THE CHRISTMAS READING

THE herald winds of Christmas sleep
High-cradled on the wooded steep.
The far stars only are a-thrill
With life; the night is cold and still.
Come, gather 'round the ingle-nook
And from its shelf take down the book
Wherein the master's genius drew
Those pictures old, but ever new;
Whose "Christmas Carol's" deathless chime
Beats down the envious touch of time.
Here let the children sit, and there
Beneath the lamp's light place thy chair.
Take, thou, the book, O! golden voice,
And read the pages of thy choice.
Tell us of Scrooge and Marley's ghost,
Of all our favorites old; but most,
Tell us with tenderness of him
We laugh and weep with—Tiny Tim.
Call thou the soul to every face
About thee in this holy place.

We shall not be ashamed at all
For frank, sweet tears you cause to fall;
But fervently, with eyelids dim
And hearts attuned to Tiny Tim,
We'll quote his words when you have done,
And say, "God bless us, every one!"

www.ingramcontent.com/pod-product-compliance
Lightning Source LLC
LaVergne TN
LVHW041617070426
835507LV00008B/287